Basic Biolog

(A primer for Access Students and

Basic Introdu

)

By Pip Flowers

Revised version 2018

Contents

The Periodic Table-an extract

1	2				3	4	5	6	7	0
$^1_1$H										
$^7_3$Li	$^9_4$Be				$^{11}_5$B	$^{12}_6$C	$^{14}_7$N	$^{16}_8$O	$^{19}_9$F	$^4_2$He / $^{20}_{10}$Ne
$^{23}_{11}$Na	$^{24}_{12}$Mg				$^{27}_{13}$Al	$^{28}_{14}$Si	$^{31}_{15}$P	$^{32}_{16}$S	$^{35}_{17}$Cl	$^{40}_{18}$Ar
$^{39}_{19}$K	$^{40}_{20}$Ca	Transition elements								

4

Chemical symbols for the first 20 elements

H hydrogen

He helium

Li lithium

Be beryllium

B boron

C carbon

N nitrogen

O oxygen

F fluorine

Ne neon

Na sodium

Mg magnesium

Al aluminium

Si silicon

P phosphorus

S sulphur (sulfur)

Cl chlorine

Ar argon

K potassium

Ca calcium

Introduction

If you are just about to return to higher level Biology study but feel you need a refresher or even a complete introduction, then this book is for you. You will find it is a bridge between where you are now and where you are going next with your studies.

This book is also for anyone with an interest in biology who wants to underpin what they read in the media with some sound background knowledge.

Whatever your aims, you can use this book in several ways; simply by reading through the sections one after another, or by using the Index of Terms page to focus on specific definitions for clarification.

I've also added optional in-depth information for those wanting to extend their knowledge.

I suggest you read the basic information before venturing into the "Going deeper…" sections at the end of each section of the book.

As with *Basic Introductions to Chemistry* this book won't get you your first Nobel Prize – but I hope it will inspire you in this; the most interesting of all subjects.

Pip Flowers.

Section 1 - Cells and cell processes

Biological Molecules - the basics in biochemistry

Let's start by looking at the macronutrients. Carbohydrates,fats,proteins.

All of these contain the elements carbon , hydrogen, oxygen. Thus, the body can take in carbohydrate, dismantle it and reassemble it as fats. However the carbon, hydrogen and oxygen are present in different proportions and arrangements. As we will also see, other substances may also be present.

A little later you will look at the structure of DNA and RNA.

Carbohydrates

The basic sub-unit or monomer of a carbohydrate is a single or simple sugar. Simple sugars such as glucose or fructose are sweet tasting. Because there's just one sub-unit we call these simple sugars "monosaccharides. Here's some extra information, the carbon, hydrogen and oxygen in simple sugars is in the ratio of 1 part carbon to 2 parts hydrogen to 1 part oxygen.

If two monosaccharides join or bond together a disaccharide is formed. The bond between the two is called a glycosidic bond. When this bonding happens, one molecule of water is released – this is called a condensation reaction. Examples of disaccharides include sucrose (the sugar you use in coffee and tea), maltose and lactose or milk sugar. Each disaccharide has different simple sugars; so sucrose is one glucose bonded to one fructose; maltose is two glucoses and lactose contains one glucose and one of a simple sugar called galactose.

Finally, simple sugars may join or bond together to form very large molecules with many saccharides. We call these 'polysaccharides. Examples are starch and cellulose -produced by plants, and glycogen found in animals and bacteria. These giant polysaccharides consist of many glucose molecules joined together by glycosidic bonds in various arrangements.

In terms of energy content; carbohydrates contain around 17-19 kJ of energy per gram.

These are examples of some common carbohydrates:

Monosaccharide	Disaccharide	Polysaccharide
Glucose	Sucrose	Starch(plants)
Fructose	Maltose	Glycogen (animals)
Galactose	Lactose	Cellulose
Ribose		

The monomers of these disaccharides are as follows:

Making disaccharides

GLUCOSE - GLUCOSE →MALTOSE

GLUCOSE - FRUCTOSE→ SUCROSE

GLUCOSE - GALACTOSE→LACTOSE

In terms of polysaccharides, note that starch, glycogen and cellulose are all made up of glucose monomers.

Fats

Fats are part of a bigger group called the lipids. The typical structure of a fat is a single molecule of a substance called glycerol, bonded with three fatty acids. The elements in fats are carbon, hydrogen and oxygen. At 37-39 kJ g, fats contain around twice the energy of carbohydrates.

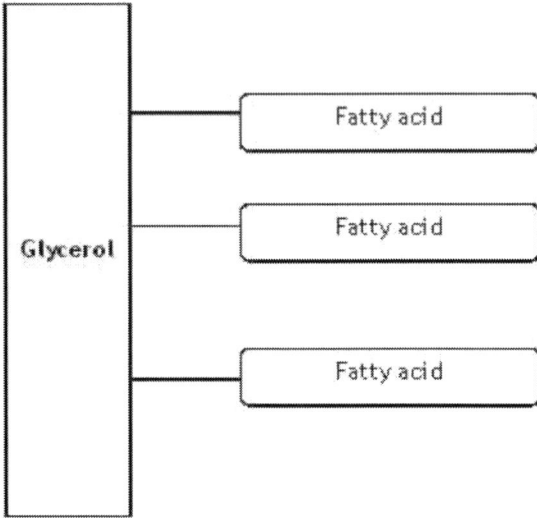

```
┌──────────┐
│          │        ┌─────────────────────┐
│          ├────────┤     Fatty acid      │
│          │        └─────────────────────┘
│          │
│          │        ┌─────────────────────┐
│ Glycerol ├────────┤     Fatty acid      │
│          │        └─────────────────────┘
│          │
│          │        ┌─────────────────────┐
│          ├────────┤     Fatty acid      │
│          │        └─────────────────────┘
└──────────┘
```

This molecule is called a triglyceride – or in some books triacylglycerol.

The bonds between the glycerol and the fatty acids form by a condensation reaction (a molecule of water is produced). They are called ester bonds.

The fatty acids dictate the characteristics of the fat. Saturated fatty acids consist of a very regular spine of carbon atoms, each bonded to 2 hydrogen atoms. If there is less hydrogen present then double bonds form between neighbouring carbons as shown below and the fat is termed 'unsaturated'.

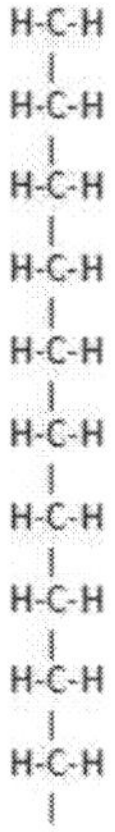
H-C-H
H-C-H
H-C-H
H-C-H
H-C-H
H-C-H
H-C-H
H-C-H
H-C-H
H-C-H

Saturated
all the
potential carbon
bonds are
taken up by
hydrogen

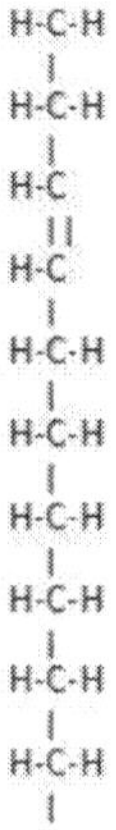
H-C-H
H-C-H
H-C
H-C
H-C-H
H-C-H
H-C-H
H-C-H
H-C-H
H-C-H

Unsaturated.
The lack of hydrogen
results in
double bonds

Overall difference- unsaturated fatty acids have less hydrogen and therefore contain one (monousaturated)or more (polyunsaturated)double bonds

That's probably a straightforward enough explanation for you at this stage. If you have some chemistry knowledge you may feel that there should be a further double bond with the next 2 carbons. A moment's thought will reassure you that these C-H bonds are covalent or sharing ones. See my ***Basic Introduction to Chemistry*** book for further information.

You may also be wondering what has happened to the oxygen. This is found at the terminal ends of the fatty acids-not shown in the above diagrams.

Proteins

Typically, protein has approximately the same energy value as carbohydrate. The sub-units (or monomers) making up proteins are amino acids. Although 20 are involved in human nutrition there are more. Amino acids join by-guess what – a condensation reaction. The bonds formed between neighbouring amino acids are called peptide bonds.

In addition to carbon,hydrogen,oxygen, amino acids always contain nitrogen and also varying amounts of sulphur. Amino acid structure is as shown below. The R group is the only difference between amino acids and gives them their distinct characteristics.

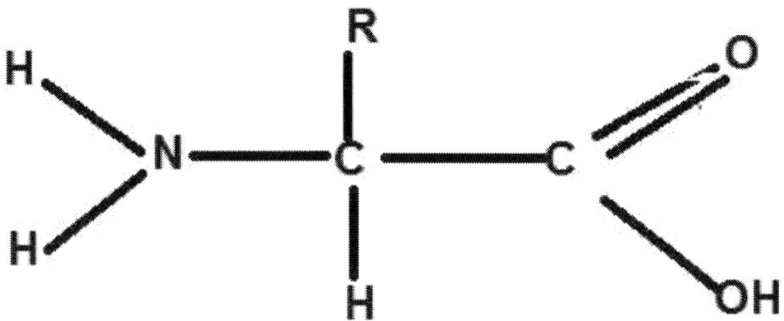

Or this can be shown as

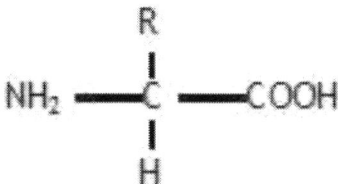

$$NH_2 - \underset{\underset{H}{|}}{\overset{\overset{R}{|}}{C}} - COOH$$

The NH$_2$ group is called the amine group and the COOH the carboxyl group.

A particular protein will have some or all of the amino acids in a unique sequence of many hundreds of monomers. The sequence of the amino acids is called the primary protein structure and comprises only of peptide bonds.

In addition to peptide bonds, further bonds can form between amino acids resulting in a spiral or helix shape or a pleated shape developing. This is known as the secondary structure of the protein. For the chemists, these further bonds are hydrogen bonds.

Yet more cross links or bonds can form between parts of the R groups of some of the amino acids, resulting in an overall globular shape developing – the tertiary structure. (For the chemists, these R group cross links may be ionic bonds, hydrogen bonds or disulphide bonds.)

Finally, there are complex proteins made up of several separate strands-this is called the quaternary structure of a protein.

Proteins carry out a huge range of functions. These can be split into two groups; structural proteins and functional proteins.

In structural proteins it is the secondary structure that is important. They are fibrous in nature and do not dissolve in water. Examples are keratin and collagen.

Functional proteins have a well developed tertiary structure-they are globular and are soluble in water and are involved in processes not structure. Examples include enzymes, hormones, and antibodies.

The shape of globular proteins is vital to their particular function. Anything that changes this shape will affect-possibly permanently ruin the protein's normal function.

Thus, increasing heat adds energy to the molecules in the protein, causing them to shift and vibrate ever more rapidly until the internal bonds break and the globular shape unravels. This is called denaturation.

Alternatively, changing the pH (acidity or alkalinity) also affects the internal (ionic) bonds. Again the protein unravels. For the chemists, this is because pH (positive Hydrogen ion concentration) relates to the electrical charge in the solution. A change in this charge also interferes with the internal electronic bonds of the protein.

Cells.. and non-cells

All living things are made up of one or more cells.

Things are regarded as living if they show any type of movement, can grow, respire, need food for energy, excrete, reproduce, show some form of sensitivity to their environment. So plants, animals, fungi, bacteria and protoctists are described as living, whereas viruses are not (see later).

Cells are living dynamic entities. As humans, all of our trillions of cells work in harmony with each other, enabling us to exhibit those characteristics of living things. Within each cell many processes are being carried out every second of the day. It's possible to see something of this activity using magnifying instruments called microscopes.

In most cases, at school or in college you will use an optical or light microscope These may allow you to magnify the image up to 400, or if you are lucky 800, 1000 times or more. This is twice the magnification of the early microscopes of Antonie van Leeuwenhoek (1632-1723), who is often called "the father of microbiology". Leeuwenhoek is credited with discovering many hitherto unknown structures, including the existence of bacteria, tiny cell structures called organelles, sperm cells and muscle fibre structure. There's plenty to see!

However electron microscopes allow a much higher magnification than even the highest quality optical microscope; many millions of times magnification in fact. The diagrams below shows the types of structures you would be able to see with an electron microscope.

Animal cell

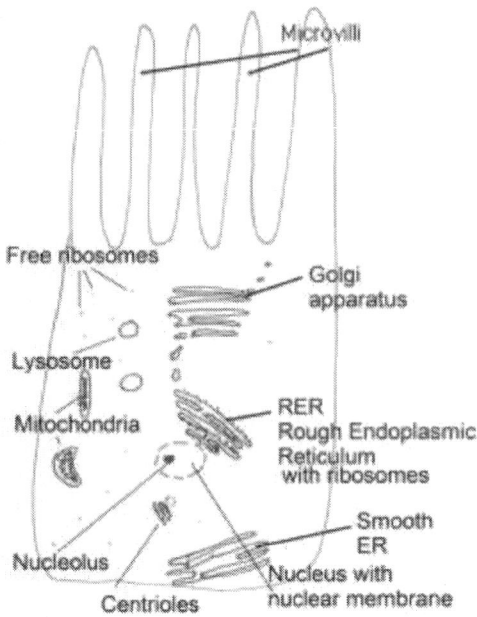

Plant cell.

Note that the organelles are displaced by the large vacuole in a plant cell.

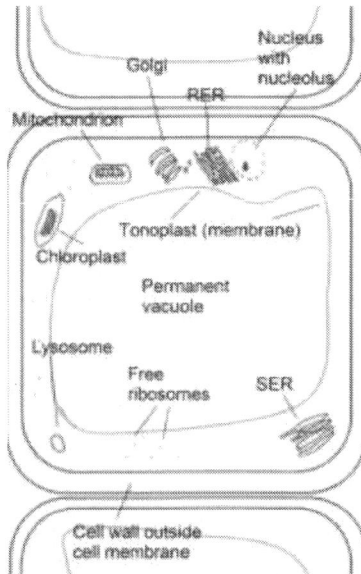

Plants, animals and fungi are collectively classed as "eukaryotes". This comes from the words "eu" – true and "karyon" – nucleus. So eukaryotic organisms have a nucleus and the other structures you can see. These minute structures within cells are called organelles. Apart from the ribosomes, the ones on the diagram are all surrounded by a membrane; another identifying characteristic of the eukaryotes.

Here is a brief rundown of what these organelles do.

Nucleus – surrounded by a membrane with pores it contains the genetic material DNA. DNA contains countless sets of instructions(genes) for countless different body functions. You will also find RNA in the nucleus (and throughout the cell). RNA acts as a messenger molecule between the genes and the ribosomes, travelling through the pores in the nuclear membrane. It is also crucial in translating DNA language into protein language.

Ribosomes – found attached to the RER (rough endoplasmic reticulum) and free in the cytoplasm. Ribosomes are the sites of protein synthesis. They do not have membranes.

Rough Endoplasmic Reticulum (RER is fine)- along with its ribosomes, is involved with the making of proteins. It also makes the Golgi Apparatus. Visualise it as sheets of lasagne (same membrane as elsewhere in the cell) studded with currants (the ribosomes).

Golgi apparatus- like RER but without ribosomes. It processes, modifies and transports proteins made by RER. It's like the finishing shop for proteins. Peroxisomes are also formed from Golgi membrane.

Smooth Endoplasmic Reticulum (SER) – like RER but without ribosomes. Involved with the making of steroids and also lipids.

Mitochondria (singular mitochondrion)- comprise two membranes. The inner one is considerably infolded. The infoldings are called cristae.

Mitochondria are the seat of most energy release. They have their own DNA (with their own genes) and their own ribosomes-smaller than the ones elsewhere in the cell. Generally believed to have been a free living prokaryotic cell which very early in evolutionary time became associated with other cells. Such cells would then have a huge energy advantage and a potential for diverse evolution.

Peroxisomes and lysosomes – both these are involved in the destruction of potentially harmful particles or substances. Peroxisomes are also important in the processing of certain fatty acids.

Centrioles-present in animals but not plants or fungi. Their role is in facilitating (mitotic) cell division. However plants and fungi manage perfectly well without them.

Chloroplasts – not found in animal cells; believed to have a similar origin to mitochondria. Contain the pigments and structures (thylakoids) needed for photosynthesis.

Cytoplasm – everything between the nuclear membrane and the cell membrane. When just describing the fluid part of this area, use the term cytosol.

Cell membrane- comprises two layers of substances called lipids, interspersed with proteins. You will find more detail in the '*Going Deeper*' section later in this book.

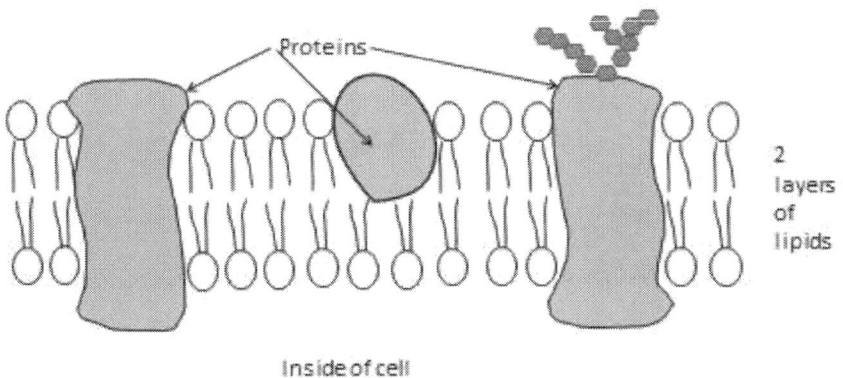

Proteins

2 layers of lipids

Inside of cell

Cell wall- found in plants (the wall is cellulose based), fungi (wall is based on a substance called chitin) and bacteria (peptidoglycan cell wall). In fungi, plants and some bacteria it lies outside the cell membrane. However other bacteria have a second membrane outside the cell wall.

Note also how plant cells have a large space called the **vacuole**- this is filled with water and solutes. It plays a part in support,transport and displaces the organelles around the edge of the plant cell as shown.

Be aware that organelles work together. The making of a protein could well involve a hormone from somewhere else in the body binding to a protein receptor on the outside of the cell membrane. This may then switch on a section of DNA in the nucleus (a gene). The gene's instructions then travel to the RER where a protein may be made. The protein is transferred to the Golgi Apparatus for final modification, which may then bud off the finished protein in a bubble of membrane (a vesicle), which then fuses with the cell's membrane before releasing the protein out of the cell into the bloodstream (via the tissue fluid). All this takes energy, which is released by the mitochondria. The whole process may take around a minute for the shorter proteins.

Prokaryotes (for our purposes bacteria)- can carry out the same cellular functions as eukaryotic cells. However they do this in specialised parts of the cytoplasm or the inner face of the cell membrane. Key differences are:

*No membrane bounded organelles or nucleus

*Smaller ribosomes

*DNA structure is different

This diagram shows four variations in basic bacterial structure.

Some species have a
second membrane outside
the cell wall

All bacteria have a cell wall
surrounding the cell membrane

Some bacteria
have flagellae for
swimming

No membrane
bounded organelles
are present

All have free
ribosomes

No nucleus-DNA in a
loop or plasmid

All have areas of membrane
specialised for various functions

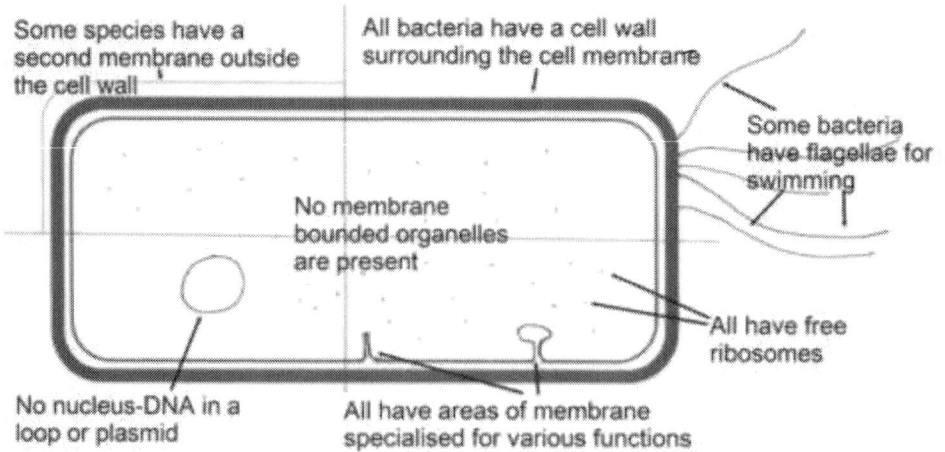

Viruses – are not generally regarded as living as they cannot carry out those living characteristics (movement, feeding etc.) on their own. Viruses infect other cells by chance. The infected cell seems to actively aid transfer of the viral genetic code into its own nucleus. The infected cell then becomes a virus factory. Viruses can be based around DNA or RNA.

Prions-are proteins folded in a particular way. They are non-living by our classification. The most notorious protein is probably the one involved with mad cow disease (in humans it causes new variant CJD, in sheep a virus causes the economically disastrous disease called scrapie). These rogue proteins seem to adversely affect normal proteins-in the latter case in the brain.

Transport in and out of cells

There is a natural tendency for molecules to move from where there are more of them to a region where there is less. Uncap a bottle of perfume and soon the vapour has filled a room. Add milk to hot tea without stirring and after a while you will finish up with a perfectly milked (possibly cold) cuppa. It works for gases and it works for fluids.

The basic reason is that all particles of every substance are in constant motion, colliding with each other and with the boundaries of their environment. Thus molecules bounce off each other and spread out over time until they are evenly distributed.

This tendency for molecules to move from a region of their high concentration to a region of low is called diffusion. Diffusion does not require any input of energy and is called a passive transport process. Diffusion can happen across cell membranes or where there is no cell membrane.

Osmosis is the process where we describe the passive movement of water down its concentration gradient across a differentially permeable membrane(but see the end of the book to refine this definition).

The rate at which diffusion movement happens is dependent on several factors including the concentration difference. This is described as the concentration gradient as shown here. The bigger the difference, the faster the substance diffuses from A to B. The substance in the left drawing would move faster than the one in the right.

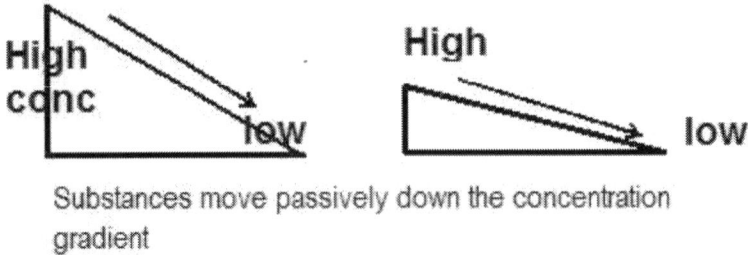

Substances move passively down the concentration gradient

However the body can't always afford to be restricted by the rate of diffusion. Special proteins in the cell membrane speed up the rate without using further energy. This is called facilitated diffusion; it happens because the membrane proteins briefly change shape and 'flick' a substance in or out of the cell. This is still passive transport- high to low concentration. Glucose is moved between cells and the bloodstream by facilitated diffusion in a lot of cases.

Quite often, cells or organelles need to accumulate substances against the concentration gradient. You will encounter plenty of examples of this.

Moving substances against the concentration gradient needs energy and is called active transport. Needless to say, cells using active transport need plenty of mitochondria.

The final transport process involves the movement of larger objects in or out of the cell. Movement out of the cell (e.g. proteins from the Golgi) is called exocytosis, movement of particles into the cell is endocytosis. Movement of liquids into the cell is called pinocytosis. Cells of the immune system may engulf and take in whole bacterial cells-this form of endocytosis is called phagocytosis.

Exo and endocytosis happen when the cell wraps the particle in a bubble or extrusion of cell membrane called a vesicle, moving it in or out of the cell by fusion with the main cell membrane-just like two soap bubbles merging then popping.

Biochemistry – enzymes

You have already discovered that enzymes are globular proteins. Enzymes are the reason we are alive! Each body process involves enzymes to ensure it happens smoothly. Enzymes make it easier for chemical reactions to occur without being used up themselves. In some way they reduce the amount of energy that would otherwise be needed to make the reaction take place. To the chemists, enzymes are biological catalysts. They are also specific to particular substances.

Enzymes may speed up the breaking down of substances (catabolic reactions-e.g. the digestion of polysaccharides into simpler sugars by the enzyme amylase), or the building up of substances (e.g. DNA from individual nucleotides by DNA polymerase).

It has been known for many years that these globular proteins have a specialised area called the "active site". The active site seems to have a concentration of R-groups. The shape of this active site is complementary to the particular substance(s) that enzyme catalyses. The substance an enzyme causes to react is called the substrate. It was recognised that specific enzymes seemed to work only with specific substrates. So, pepsin (a protein digesting enzyme)never worked with starch.

It's also been known that somehow when the active site of enzyme binds with its similarly shaped substrate, either the substrate breaks down (catabolic) or is added to (anabolic).

For years this was known as the 'lock and key' model. The diagram below shows the basic idea of an exact match between enzyme and substrate.

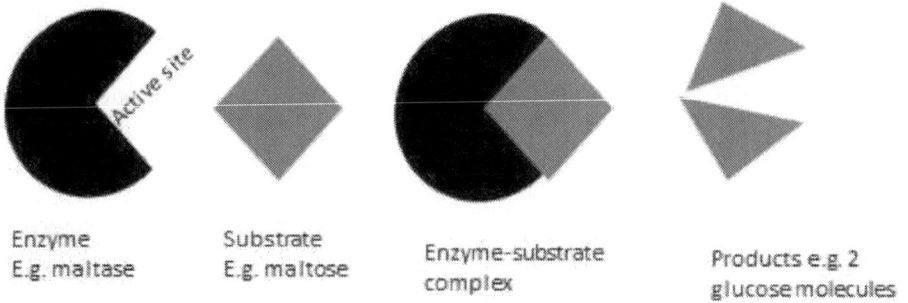

Enzyme
E.g. maltase

Substrate
E.g. maltose

Enzyme-substrate
complex

Products e.g. 2
glucose molecules

A few years ago it became obvious that this very rigid model didn't match reality, so now the model is that of an induced fit. The theory is that enzyme and substrate bind loosely but then the enzyme protein deforms to fit tightly round the substrate and exerts force on it causing the catabolic/anabolic reaction to take place more easily.

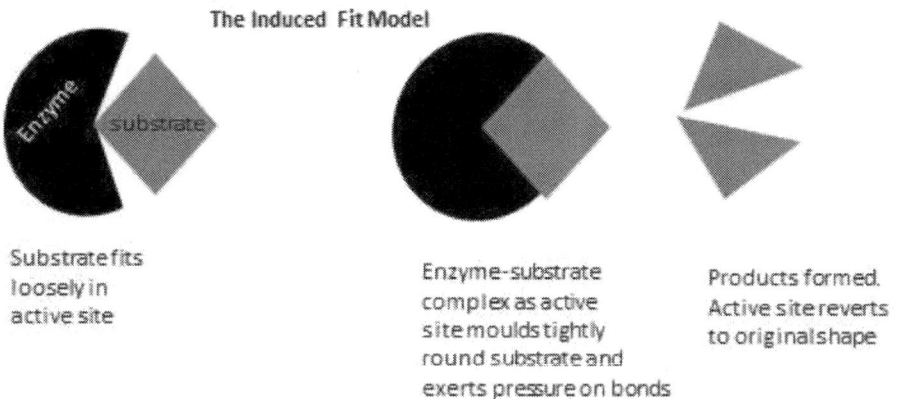

The Induced Fit Model

Substrate fits
loosely in
active site

Enzyme-substrate
complex as active
site moulds tightly
round substrate and
exerts pressure on bonds

Products formed.
Active site reverts
to original shape

This has led to the suggestion that while some enzymes are very specific- others are less so and due to induced fit can adjust to a range of reasonably similar shaped substrates. Science moves on.

Note also that being proteins, enzymes are affected by pH and temperature. The section on proteins explained why this is.

Biochemistry – DNA and RNA

Everybody these days has heard about DNA. A few less know it's something to do with each individual's unique genetic profile. Fewer still have heard about RNA. Let's fill in the gaps.

First DNA. DNA is a big – very big molecule. Like proteins, fats and carbohydrates it is made up of many, many subunits. The subunits of DNA are called nucleotides. Each nucleotide has three parts, a sugar, a phosphate and something called a base.

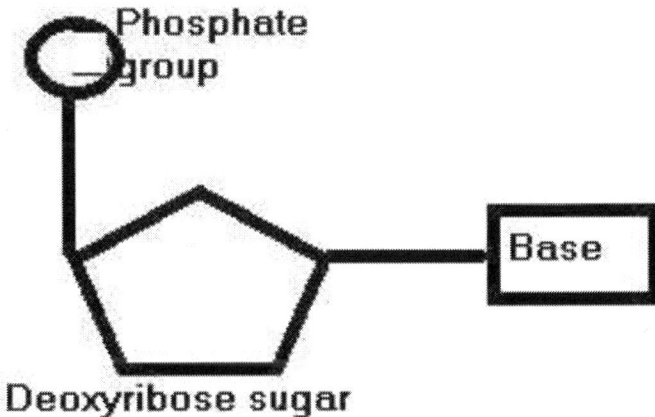

The phosphate and sugars are the same throughout. However there are four different bases in DNA represented by the letters A (adenine), T (thymine), G (guanine) and C (cytosine).

Nucleotides join phosphate to sugar lengthways to form a long strand, and base to base to form a second strand as shown.

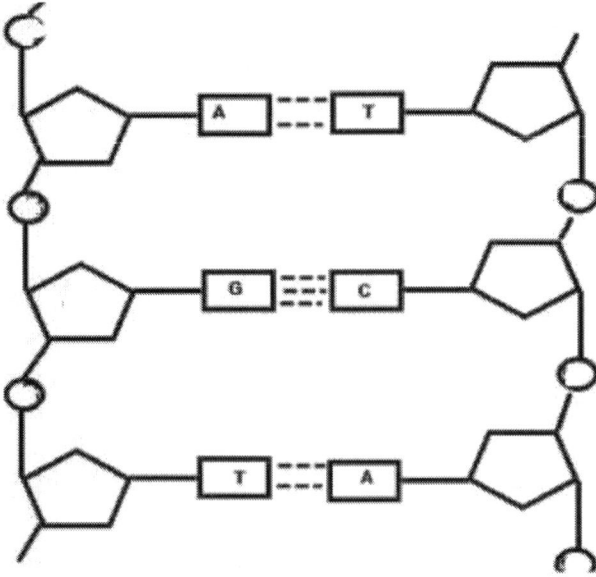

Notice several points;

- The strands run in opposite directions

- A bonds with T but never with G or C

- G and C will bond but never with A or T

The A-T and G-C pairing are known as the base pairing rules- you will find more information later in *'Going deeper'*. RNA is also a polynucleotide genetic molecule-but with a difference. Although it has the bases A,C,G, there is no thymine (T) present. Instead of T, RNA has uracil (U). The same base pairing rules apply-although RNA normally pairs with part of a DNA strand to trigger protein synthesis.

Other RNA/DNA differences are that RNA occurs throughout the cell; in the nucleus as mRNA, in ribosomes on RER and also free ribosomes found in the cytoplasm and as tRNA. Also that RNA is a shorter molecule than DNA.

DNA is able to replicate itself in order to produce enough new DNA when cells are to divide. DNA and RNA work together when the gene for making a protein is switched on. Neither of these topics will be explored in this book.

Metabolic reactions - Cell Respiration

Animals eat food in order to obtain energy and nutrients. The process of digestion progressively breaks the food down into smaller and smaller fragments. Carbohydrates are broken down into single glucose molecules. These can then be broken down in the body's cells to release energy.

The breaking down of glucose in body cells is called **CELL RESPIRATION**. Here is a simplified step-by-step account of what happens:

Glucose is carried from the digestive system in the blood supply to the cells of the body. Once inside the cell, the glucose is broken down in three stages.

Stage 1 – glycolysis

In the first stage (glycolysis), glucose is broken down to the substance pyruvate(sometimes called pyruvic acid). A little energy is released during this process, at the end of which there are two possibilities, depending on whether or not oxygen is available:

 (a) If OXYGEN is not present (cell is "anaerobic"), no further energy can be produced and cell respiration stops. The pyruvate is turned to lactate(lactic acid). This "word equation" describes the process:

GLUCOSE $\rightarrow\rightarrow$ A little energy + Lactic Acid + Carbon Dioxide

OR

   (b) If OXYGEN is present("aerobic" cell respiration) the way is open for much more energy to be released from the glucose in two further steps as follows.

Stage 2 -The Krebs Cycle.
The pyruvate is processed inside the cell's mitochondria. This releases a further small amount of energy.

Stage 3 - The Electron Transport Chain (ETC for short)
A further chain of reactions takes place in the mitochondria releasing the majority of the energy, which is promptly temporarily locked up in the chemical substance ATP. The word equation for aerobic cell respiration is:

GLUCOSE + OXYGEN →→ENERGY+CARBON DIOXIDE+WATER

The term 'oxidative phosphorylation' relates to this stage, which results in the vast majority of ATP production.

Going deeper with cells

The cell membrane is a complex structure. Here's a more detailed view.

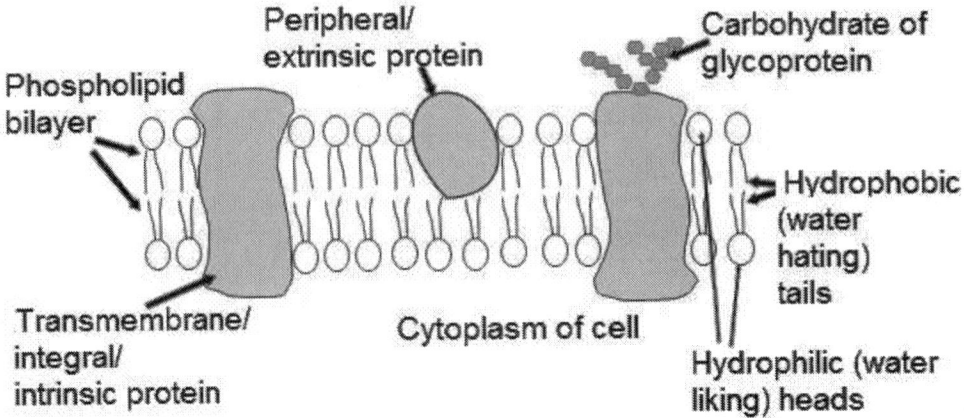

The lipid tails are repelled by water, whereas the lipid heads are attracted to it. As cell membranes separate watery compartments the bilayer is naturally orientated as shown.

Proteins may span the complete membrane (transmembrane/integral/intrinsic proteins) or occur in the outer layer (peripheral or extrinsic proteins). The latter may be of short term duration.

Proteins are involved in a range of transport processes. Some are associated with carbohydrate groups (glycoproteins); these groups are important in signalling between cells and also enable recognition by the white blood cells of the immune system.

The membrane itself is a fluid structure-proteins may ebb and flow from one place to another in the fluid phospholipid layers. This is called the fluid-mosaic model.

In bacterial (prokaryotic) cells, some species have a second membrane outside the cell wall as shown below:

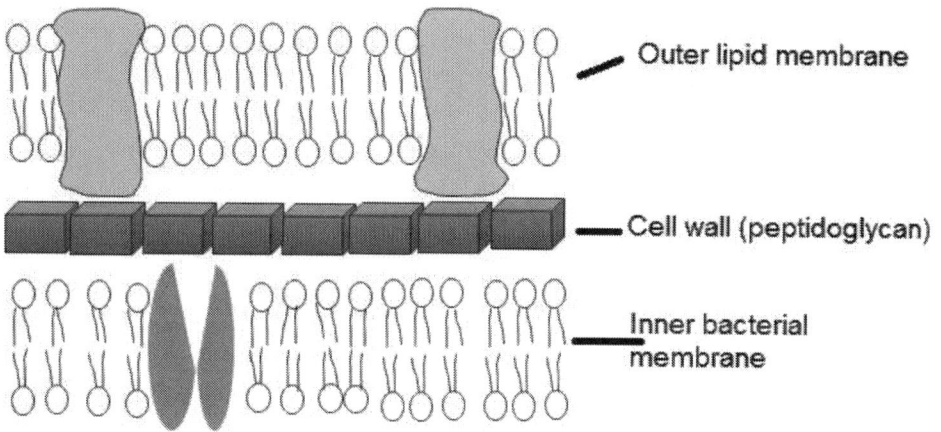

Outer lipid membrane

Cell wall (peptidoglycan)

Inner bacterial membrane

This feature is used when identifying bacterial species. In Gram-Staining a purple "Gram" stain is added to the bacterial sample, penetrating the outer layer. The sample is then washed with ethanol which dissolves lipids. A second red stain is then added.

Species with the outer membrane lose the purple stain and appear red under the microscope. They are called Gram negative. Species with just the cell wall are unaffected and retain the Gram (purple) stain. They are called Gram positive.

The fact that bacterial DNA is not enclosed by a membrane means that plasmids can readily be used by scientists carrying out genetic engineering. It is now relatively straightforward to splice a human gene (e.g. the insulin gene) into a plasmid, reinsert the plasmid into a new bacterial cell which can then be cultured to produce millions of new bacteria all synthesising huge quantities of pure human insulin at modest cost.

Going deeper with Transport

It's no longer acceptable to talk about water molecule concentration when describing osmosis. So the old definitions along the lines of; "Osmosis is the movement of water from a region of high water molecule concentration to low across a differentially permeable membrane" are strictly taboo.

Instead, definitions may say; "Osmosis describes the movement of water from a region of high solute concentration to a region of low across a differentially permeable membrane". By definition, if there are a lot of solute molecules there will be fewer water molecules per unit volume.

It is also possible (and desirable) to quantify osmotic descriptions by introducing the idea of water potential. This is represented by the symbol Ψ. Water potential describes the overall tendency of any water molecules present to move.

Pure water is given a water potential value of 0. Solutes reduce the ability of water molecules to move – thus the more solutes present the more negative a solution becomes. A red blood cell contains dissolved substances and therefore has a negative water potential. If the cell is placed in distilled water with a water potential of zero, water moves into the more negative region (the cell) and will burst it.

This provides another definition for osmosis based on water potential; "Osmosis describes the movement of water molecules (from a less negative) to a more negative region of water potential" OR less desirably "Osmosis describes the movement of water molecules from a region of higher to a region of lower water potential".

The following diagram shows how facilitated diffusion occurs.

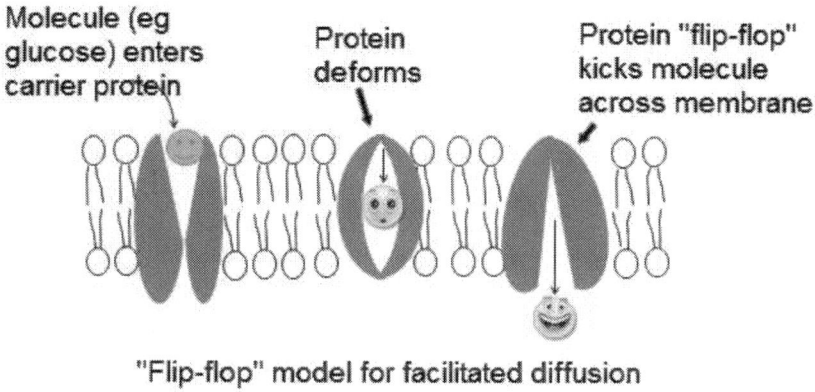

"Flip-flop" model for facilitated diffusion

Going deeper with DNA and RNA

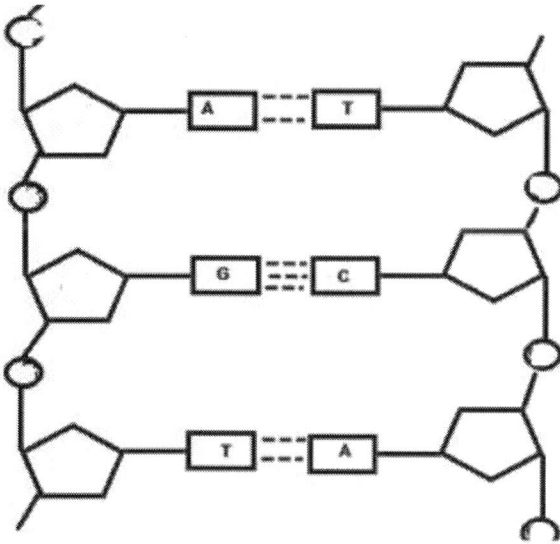

The dotted lines represent comparatively weak hydrogen bonds linking the bases. Two bonds link A-T and three link C-G.

The reason that neither T and G nor A and C customarily bond is that A and G are both larger than T and C as shown.

33

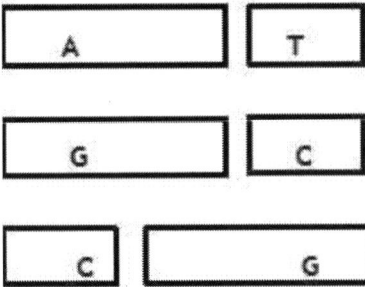

This enables a strictly parallel two stranded molecule. However if irregular pairing occurs-the following could result:

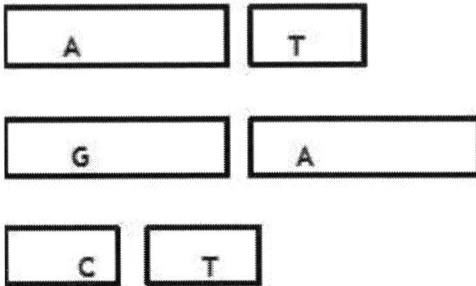

This structure is no longer parallel and the lengthways (ester) bonds and the hydrogen bonds would be placed under tension and become unstable.

Going Deeper into Cell Respiration

In fact aerobic respiration has hundreds of reactions. One reason that it is a stepwise process is that if all the energy was released from glucose at once, the heat generated would damage the cell machinery. In addition to glucose, energy can also be released from amino acids and fatty acids.

The account in this e-book and many textbooks identifies three main stages; Glycolysis-Krebs Cycle-Electron Transport Chain.

However many books now include a further process called the Link Reaction between Glycolysis and the Krebs Cycle. You may also see the Krebs Cycle called the Citric Acid Cycle or the TCA Cycle; while the final process involving the Electron Transport Chain is called Oxidative Phosphorylation.

The energy released (and used) in the process is stored in the chemical form ATP (adenosine triphosphate). ATP can be formed and broken down almost instantly from ADP (adenosine diphosphate) to store and release energy respectively.

Here is some further information about each of the stages.

Glycolysis.

Glucose enters the cell by facilitated diffusion. Glucose has 6 carbon atoms per molecule.

Glucose needs an energetic 'push start' from stored cell ATP. Two ATP's are used to "phosphorylate" each glucose molecule.

This results in the formation of fructose bisphosphate, which is split into two 3-carbon molecules of triose phosphate or glyceraldehyde-3-phosphate (GALP) which is then converted into pyruvate. There are many other intermediate substances in this process. By the end of glycolysis some ATP has been generated creating a net gain of two ATP's. Glycolysis also liberates hydrogen which is mopped up by the substance NAD, reducing NAD to NADH. NAD is called a hydrogen acceptor.

Link Reaction.

The pyruvate is actively transported into the mitochondrial matrix (think of the cytoplasm of the mitochondrion). The pyruvate combines with the substance coenzyme A to give acetyl coenzyme A (acetyl CoA). Carbon dioxide and hydrogen are released. The carbon dioxide is released into the bloodstream to be breathed out. The hydrogen is again mopped up by NAD for later use.

The Krebs Cycle/Citric Acid Cycle/TCA Cycle

Acetyl CoA combines with oxaloacetic acid to form citric acid... a series of reactions then liberates more hydrogen (again mopped up by NAD) as well as carbon dioxide (ultimately breathed out). The removal of CO_2 and H regenerates oxaloacetic acid for next ACoA molecule. Overall you can expect a net gain of 2 ATP's from the Krebs Cycle.

The Electron Transport Chain

This is where the majority of the energy is released and the most ATP formed from ADP.

The hydrogen previously 'mopped up' by NADH is now released and split into protons and electrons (H^+ and e^-). The Basic Introductions to Chemistry book explains what protons and electrons are.

The inner mitochondrial membrane has carrier molecules, the electrons pass from one carrier molecule to the next releasing energy as they transfer.

The energy drives an active transport pump located in the inner mitochondrial membrane. This is called a proton pump.

The proton pump transports H+ into the intermembrane space-creating a high concentration of hydrogen there. Hydrogen cannot diffuse across this membrane back into the matrix because the membrane is impermeable. Except via protein channels termed 'stalked particles'.

The stalked particles are lined with an enzyme (an ATPase or ATP synthase or ATP synthetase depending on your book!) which can make ATP from ADP.

As the H^+ diffuses down its gradient back through stalked particles into the mitochondrial matrix the movement activates the ATPase forming ATP.

This is called the chemiosmotic model.

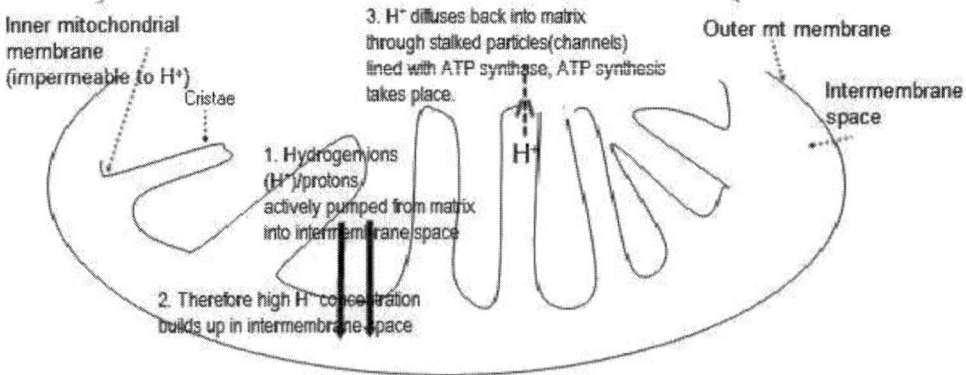

The overall balance of ATP production per molecule of glucose is as follows- but note the figures vary according to the substrate and mitochondrial efficiency.

	ATP used	ATP synthesised	Net ATP produced
Glycolysis	2	4	2
Link Reaction	0	0	0
Kreb's Cycle	0	2	2
Electron Transport Chain (oxidative phosphorylation)	0	34	34
		Potential net yield of ATP	38

Section 2 – Organs and organ processes

The circulatory system – structure and layout

Organisms need some way of getting oxygen from the air to the place where cell respiration takes place. Animals typically have circulatory systems to carry gases in their bodies. The next few sections will concentrate on the mammalian-mainly human-circulatory system. Systems with blood vessels (e.g. arteries, veins, capillaries) are called **closed circulatory systems**. But there are lots of variations.

Some organisms don't need a system- small organisms (e.g. unicellular ones), or those with a high surface area to internal volume ratio (e.g. flatworms) satisfy their oxygen needs through diffusion into their structure. We are not concerned with these organisms in this section. What follows relates to metazoans (multi celled organisms).

Some organisms have a system without blood vessels- This is called an **open circulatory system** arthropods (a huge group including insects, spiders, crustaceans) essentially have blood contained 'loose' within the body cavity. Oxygen in the 'blood' bathes the internal organs and tissues, enabling respiration. Carbon dioxide is removed similarly. Note that the blood is not the same as our blood. It is a mixture of blood and other fluids and is called haemolymph.

There are different types of 'pump'- higher animals have the familiar heart. Organisms with open circulatory systems have many permutations. In some cases body movement aids circulation, in insects there are tubular hearts found linking the blood in the body cavity to the head. Squids have three hearts!

Hearts vary- in higher animals with closed systems hearts may have 2, 3 or 4 chambers. Fish may have 2 or 3 chambers, frogs and lizards 3. Mammals, crocodiles and birds all have 4 chambered hearts.

One loop or two? Two types of closed system

Single Circulatory System	Double Circulatory System

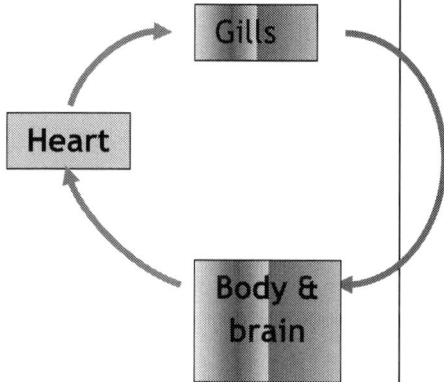

In fish, the blood is pumped from the heart to the gills where it receives oxygen from the water by diffusion. The oxygen is delivered to the body tissues, picks up carbon dioxide and returns to the heart for the next pumping cycle.

Disadvantage-loss of pressure as blood passes through narrow blood vessels in the gills means a slow delivery to the body tissues. This limits aerobic respiration. This limits the ability to thermoregulate internally. Fish are 'cold blooded'…. which suits them fine.

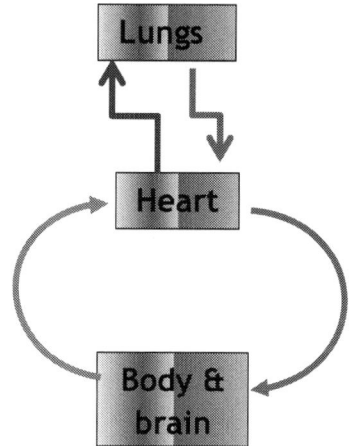

Mammals and birds need more oxygen to release sufficient energy (by cell respiration) for warming up and cooling down.

The low pressure oxygenated blood from the lungs gets an extra boost from the heart, so that oxygenated blood is delivered at full pressure to the body's organs and tissues. Note that the heart handles oxygenated AND deoxygenated blood in the double system. The oxygenating loop from heart to lungs and back to the heart is the **pulmonary circulation**

The loop from heart to body and back to heart is the **systemic circulation**.

The following diagram gives a slightly more detailed view of some of the main pathways in the human system. You are strongly recommended to learn the names and locations of all these blood vessels by heart. It will help you do this by doing a quick sketch like the following one!

The human circulatory system- showing some key blood vessels

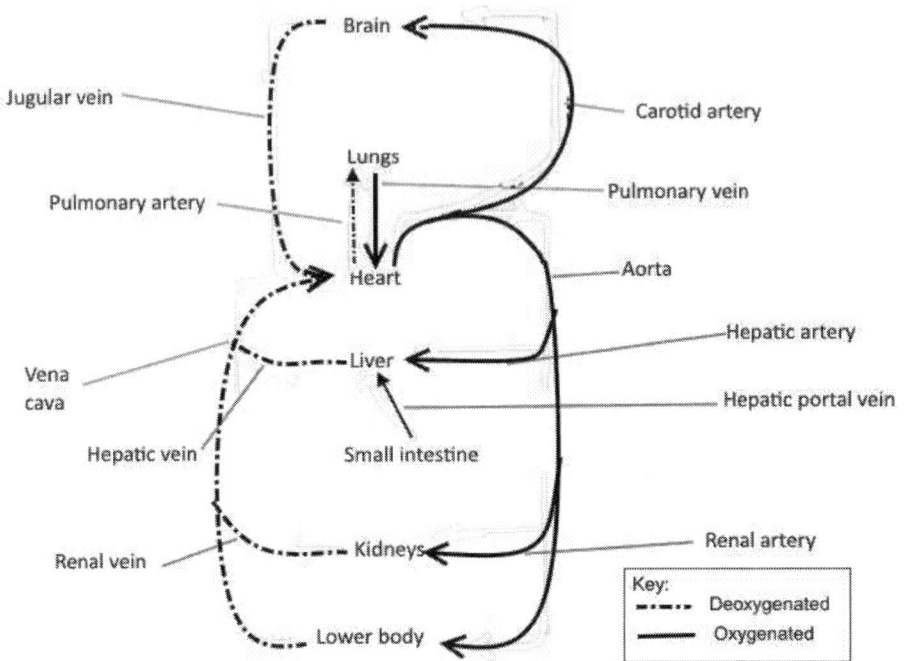

The circulatory system – blood vessel structure

Blood vessel types are:

Arteries- always carry blood AWAY from the heart, whether oxygenated or deoxygenated. The aorta is the biggest artery; the arterial sub branches from it then divide and subdivide into small arteries called arterioles, then into capillaries.

The walls of arteries are (should) be impermeable.

Capillaries- tiny blood vessels maybe 7-8 µm in diameter (that is 7/1000 of one mm). These are concerned with exchange of gasses and nutrients between blood and the body's cells. The walls are just one layer of (squamous) cells thick. In other words they are pure tunica interna and nothing else.

Veins – return blood to the heart from capillaries, which merge into small veins called venules, which merge into the veins and ultimately the vena cava.

This picture was taken using a camera phone looking down the eyepiece of a microscope. It shows a section of an artery prepared by one of my students. (100x magnification)

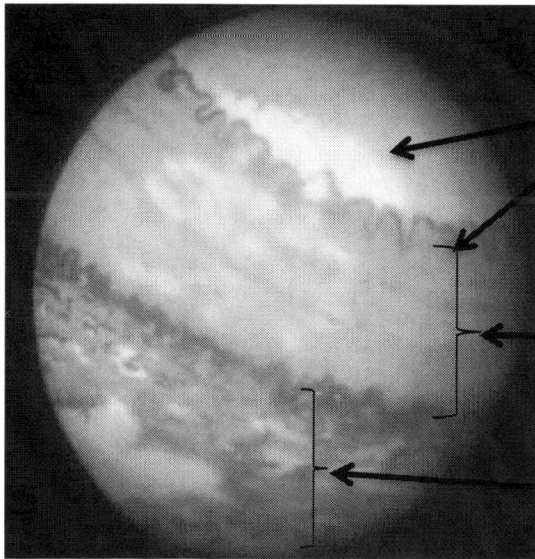

Lumen-the cavity the blood flows along
Endothelium-single layer of squamous cells giving a smooth surface for blood flow. Together with its supporting connective tissue it makes up the **tunica interna (or intima)**

Tunica media-the middle layer of an artery. Mainly elastic fibres and muscle.

Tunica externa-the outermost layer. Mainly elastic fibres and collagen for strength.

Conducting arteries

The arteries closest to the heart have to withstand the greatest pressure due to the heart's pumping. The have thick walls with much elastic tissue to allow the walls of the arteries to stretch and recoil with each spurt of blood from the heart. Notice the 'wrinkly' appearance of the endothelium in the above picture. Not surprisingly, this artery is no longer under pressure. The elastic recoil also helps urge blood along when the heart relaxes between beats (the windkessel effect). These elastic arteries are known as 'conducting arteries'.

Distributing arteries

Further from the heart the arteries are able to contract and relax in order to divert blood to where it is need. As the pressure is less, they have less elastic tissue but a lot of muscle tissue. These are circular muscles; by contracting they reduce the blood flow. For this reason they are known as muscular or distributing arteries.

The capillary bed

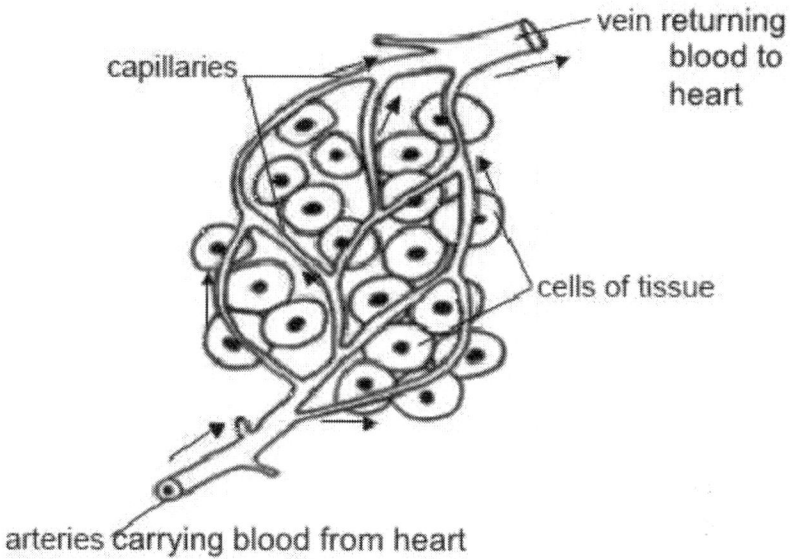

There are three types of capillary, sinusoidal, continuous and fenestrated. For now just appreciate that the permeable nature of these tiny vessels makes it possible for fluids and gases to be exchanged between blood and tissues. Of which more later.

Veins

As the blood travels further and further away from the heart the pressure drops. Partly due to the distance from the pumping action of the heart, partly due to the "friction" or peripheral resistance as the blood flows a long way along narrow blood vessels.

The blood pressure is at its lowest in the veins. Veins have less muscle and elastic tissue than arteries. They also have very thin walls that can be squeezed by skeletal muscle, thus aiding the flow of blood back to the heart (the toothpaste tube effect). Valves help ensure that blood does not flow backwards under the influence of gravity (e.g. in the legs).

The circulatory system – the heart: structure and function

Diagram of the human heart

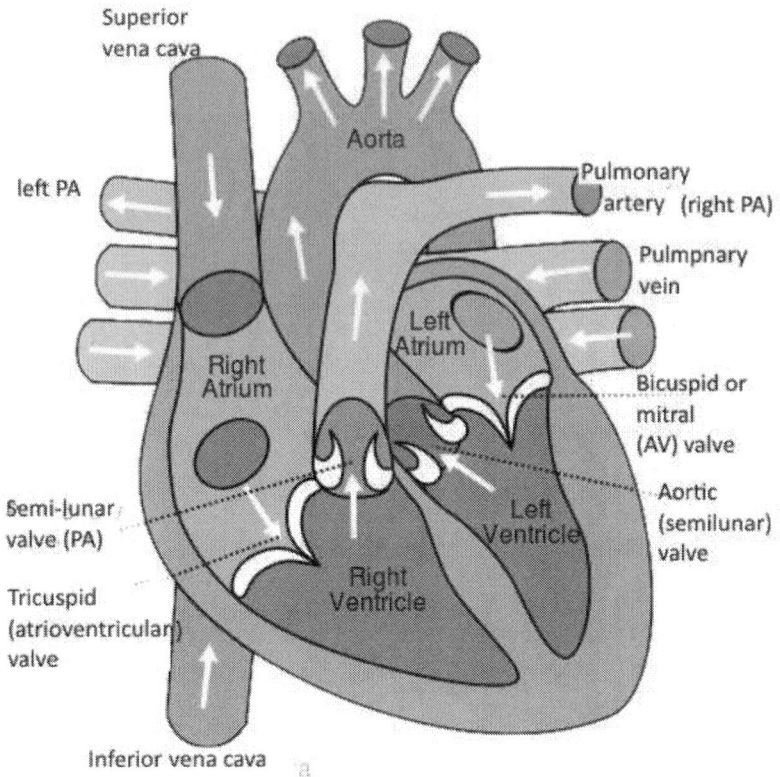

Superior vena cava
Aorta
left PA
Pulmonary artery (right PA)
Pulmpnary vein
Left Atrium
Right Atrium
Bicuspid or mitral (AV) valve
Semi-lunar valve (PA)
Aortic (semilunar) valve
Left Ventricle
Tricuspid (atrioventricular) valve
Right Ventricle
Inferior vena cava

The tricuspid and bicuspid valves are reinforced by tendons (not shown) linking the valves to knots of muscle in the heart wall (papillary muscle). The tendons help to prevent the valves flipping inside out under the high pressure that is exerted when the ventricles contract.

The human heart is myogenic. Myogenic means that heart tissue has its own inbuilt rhythm, causing regular contractions that we call the heartbeat. This is unlike the neurogenic hearts of some species (e.g. squids). Neurogenic hearts are stimulated by firing signals from the brain or central nervous system.

This is how the human heart works.

A specialised knot of tissue called the SA node (sino-atrial node or simply SAN) is located in the wall of the right atrium. All through your life, the SA node is sending tiny electrical signals across the atrial muscle as shown on the diagram.

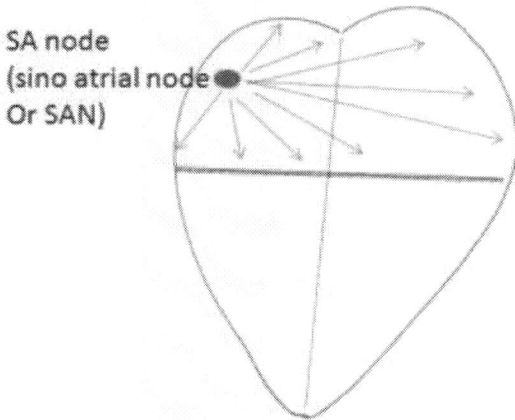

SA node
(sino atrial node
Or SAN)

The electrical impulses cause the atria to contract. This squeezes the blood through the atrioventricular valves into the ventricles. We call this stage atrial systole.

The impulses from the SA node can only pass to the ventricular muscle via one point, called the AV node (atrio-ventricular or AVN).

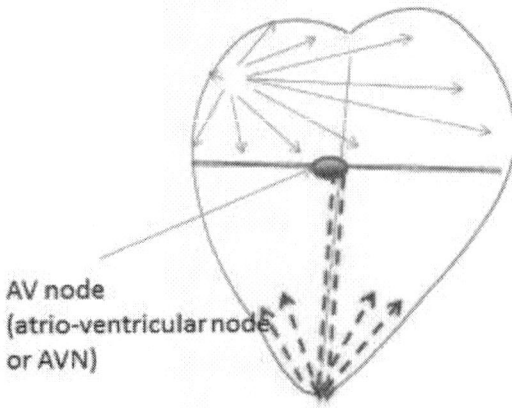

AV node
(atrio-ventricular node
or AVN)

The AV node stores up these impulses and then releases them down special conducting fibres (Purkyne/Purkinje fibres contained within a bundle called the Bundle of His) in a very fast burst.

When the impulses reach the ventricles, they cause them to contract very strongly from the base upwards. This forces the blood out of the heart towards the lungs from the right ventricle and the body from the left ventricle. The ventricular contraction(ventricular systole) causes an increase in pressure forcing the one way atrioventricular valves shut and the semi lunar valves open.

Finally the heart relaxes – (ventricular) diastole. During this stage deoxygenated blood from the body is trickling through the right atrium into the right ventricle. Oxygenated blood is doing the same from the lungs in the left chambers of the heart.

The firing of the SA and AV nodes can be detected using an ECG.

The circulatory system: ECGs and Pressure traces

This diagram shows a typical ECG trace.

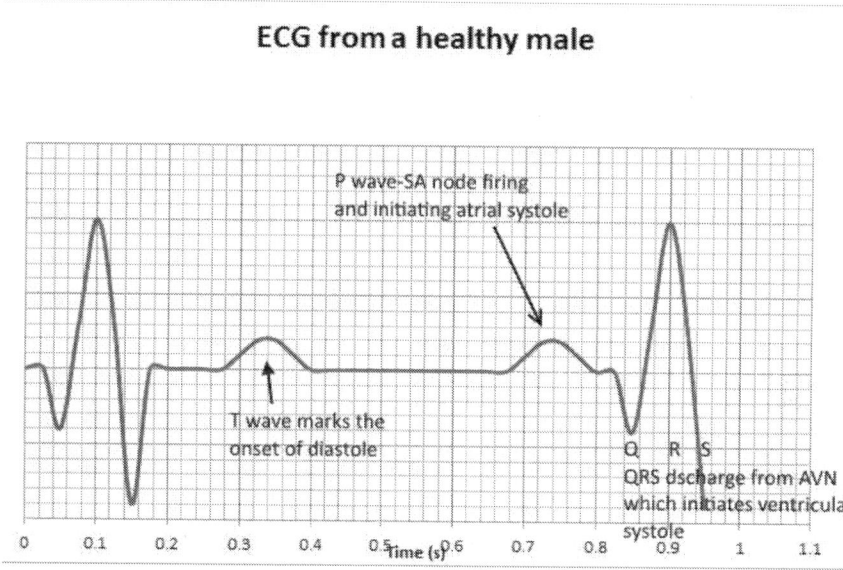

ECG from a healthy male

P wave-SA node firing and initiating atrial systole

T wave marks the onset of diastole

Q R S

QRS dscharge from AVN which inibiates ventricular systole

Time (s)

0   0.1   0.2   0.3   0.4   0.5   0.6   0.7   0.8   0.9   1   1.1

The cardiac pressure changes are shown on the following pressure trace.

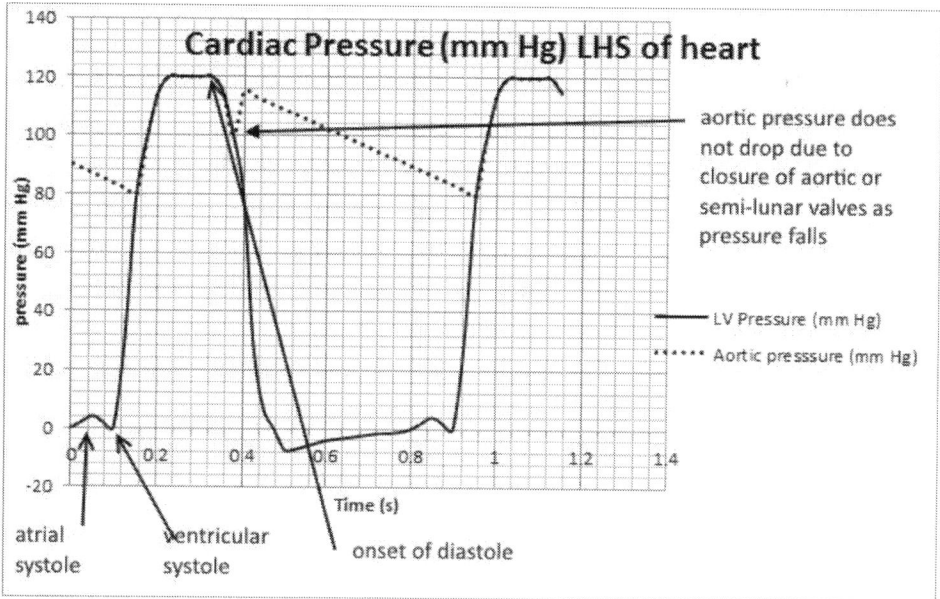

Cardiac Pressure (mm Hg) LHS of heart

pressure (mm Hg)

aortic pressure does not drop due to closure of aortic or semi-lunar valves as pressure falls

LV Pressure (mm Hg)

Aortic presssure (mm Hg)

Time (s)

atrial systole

ventricular systole

onset of diastole

The relationship between the electrical and physical events of the cardiac cycle is shown here.

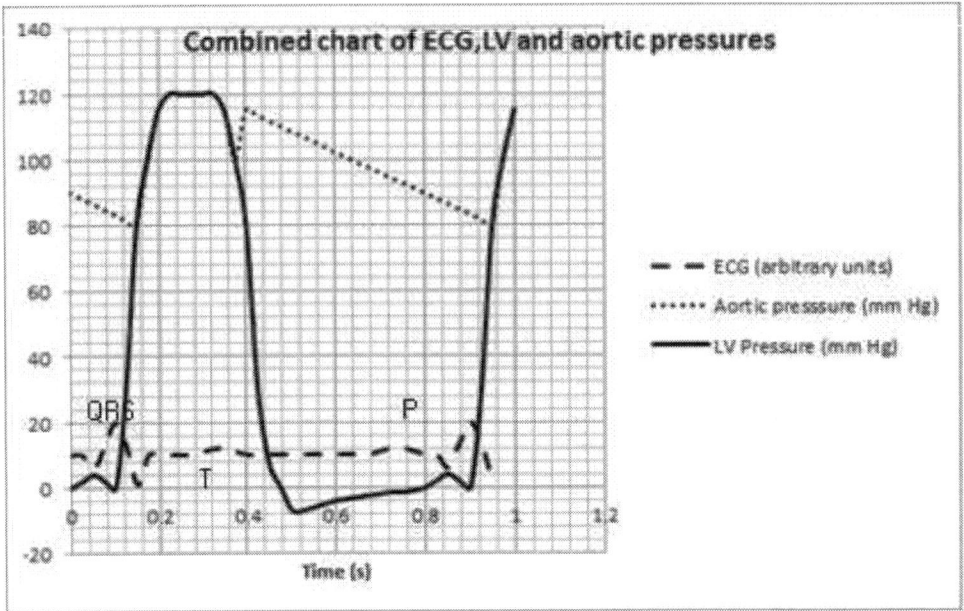

Combined chart of ECG, LV and aortic pressures

Legend:
- – – ECG (arbitrary units)
- •••••• Aortic presssure (mm Hg)
- —— LV Pressure (mm Hg)

Time (s)

Exam questions often test your understanding of these parameters. There are some examples in the latest Quickfire Questions series I have produced on Amazon.

Index of terms

Further Reading

I hope this book has helped introduce you into biological study. If it has whetted your appetite for more, try my other books.

1. Basic Introductions to Biology - Book 2 Digestion, blood sugar regulation and the role of the kidneys (paperback)
2. Basic Introductions to Biology – Microbiology,immunity and anti-microbial medications. (paperback or e-book)
3. Quickfire Revision Questions for Biology (Book 1)
4. Quickfire Revision Questions for Biology(Book 2-going deeper)
5. Basic Introductions to Biology- Book 3 Kidneys, structure and functions (e-book format for Kindle)
6. Basic Introductions to Biology – Digestion, blood sugar and diabetes (e-book)
7. A basic introduction to Chemistry (e-book)

Acknowledgements

Heart diagram from https://commons.wikimedia.org/wiki/File%3ADiagram_of_the_human_heart_(cropped).svg [accessed 26/07/15] Creative Commons Attribution-Share Alike 3.0 Unported license

Capillary bed diagram attribution to By Sunshineconnelly at en.wikibooks [CC BY 3.0 (http://creativecommons.org/licenses/by/3.0)], from Wikimedia Commons

Printed in Great Britain
by Amazon